DECOMPRESS

A 7 DAY GUIDE TO:

reduce stress, anxiety, and depression.

JOANNE HADJIA

Design and layout for cover by Ricky Cribb

Published by Djia Media Publishing
Los Angeles California
First published 2019

ISBN 978-0-6486846-0-2

Disclaimer: *This guided book is not intended to replace or overwrite the advice of psychologists, counselors, therapists, psychiatrists or any other forms of medical and therapeutic advice. I am not a qualified or licensed healthcare professional and cannot guarantee any results or changes. If you are feeling depressed or having suicidal thoughts please contact a healthcare professional urgently.*

Table of Contents

DEDICATION & ACKNOWLEDGEMENT

I want to dedicate this book to my parents, Louise Barry and Mario Hadjia. Who combined, taught me the right balance of being feisty and calm. They gave me the courage to chase what I'm passionate about, the discipline to finish what I start despite the setbacks, the bravery to defend what I believe is right, the decency to respect all people and the certainty of knowing who I am regardless of others' opinions. Without your magic, I wouldn't have written this book. Thank you for supporting me even when my choice of path in life seemed unlikely. Above all, thank you for showing my sisters and I - your 4 daughters - that true love does exist yah cute little old couple, haaaha!

INTRODUCTION

Let's get right to it. You've been feeling shitty lately, and it definitely sucks. Maybe you've felt that horrible heaviness after a breakup, a bad test result, a loss of money, or perhaps a disappointment from a business deal. Maybe you have noticed you're feeling shitty more often with less obvious reasons as to why you're feeling that way. That is a scary feeling! It isn't scary to be unhappy when you have an obvious reason to be but it's scary to feel unhappy and truly not know what is causing that unhappiness.

I bet you've wondered why you don't feel content when there are people around the world who seem to be going through much worse, yet somehow appear to be happier than you. Happiness seems to be apparent in their lives whilst you keep feeling down, tired, and anxious. Why is this? All you know is: *Surely, this isn't the way life is meant to be.* Let me start by telling you that life is not meant to feel impossible every step of the way and this guide may help kick-start you in the right direction towards inner happiness!

Life isn't meant to feel heavy on your shoulders. While little ups and downs in your mood are natural, you shouldn't be feeling unsatisfied regularly. We all know contrast in life helps us appreciate the good days from the bad. How else would we know how great it is to wake up feeling excited if we hadn't experienced a bunch of demotivated challenging days? We should embrace contrast and use it to better understand ourselves.

We have all felt sad at some point and been so thankful to feel like ourselves again once it passes. We suddenly really appreciate the good days. On the other hand, we have all had a blocked nose and instantly wished for our regular health back that we took for granted every night when we're trying to sleep. These opposites experiences of good and bad help us be appreciative, however it is up to us to acknowledge the good times without requiring constant negative experiences as a harsh reminder! We have the ability to take on the difficult moments, no matter how challenging, and learn from them. We are not meant to carry the negativity around permanently, allowing life to weigh us down.

For the next 7 days, let's see how far you can shift your mood to start appreciating life from a positive place more consistently. Imagine feeling content, peaceful, and calm throughout your day! Imagine how amazing it would feel to have more control over your emotions, to become more patient and less bothered when things don't go as planned. If that is something you truly are ready to achieve, you must complete the 7 daily steps to really magnify your potential. It is surprisingly empowering to realize how much more control you have over your life when you put in the effort to stay consistent. It's time to decompress!

This page was intentionally left blank

DIARY LOG INTRO

This is your chance to be as real as you can get with yourself on a dedicated and private page that no one needs to see. Write down everything about what you're feeling and don't shy away from mentioning what is bothering and upsetting you. Write if you have felt let down, hurt, depressed, anxious or lost. Let it all out! Write down everything - memories or detailed events explaining what you'd like to work through, or who you'd like to get along better with, or what you'd like to achieve. This is your opportunity to let a little energy out - be as messy as you like.

You will be able to come back to this, to reflect on how you felt and to monitor any progress. At the end of this 7 day guide, you will have another chance to write an outro diary to compare any changes.

....
....
....
....
....
....
....
....
....

....
....
....
....
....
....
....
....
....
....
....
....
....
....
....
....
....
....
....
....
....
....
....
....
....
....

....
....
....
....
....
....
....
....
....
....
....
....
....
....
....
....
....
....
....
....
....
....
....
....
....
....
....
....
....
....

OVERVIEW OF
DAILY BREAKDOWN

Morning Read [less than 7 minutes]

Each day you will start off by reading a short informative chapter. When I say start off, I seriously meant start off! This guide needs to be next to your bed, on top of your phone, so you cannot make the excuse that you forgot and started checking your texts and social media notifications first. Don't worry, the chapter will take you less than 7 minutes to read! It won't drag on and feel like you're in school with extra homework.

Morning Meditation - Music Supplied

https://lnk.to/learningenergy

If you're new to meditation, don't freak out! This isn't meant to make you feel like you're walking among hippies, wearing crystals and birthstones, burning sage and tattooing chakras on your body while reading the stars (although I love all that, haha). This is a short 7 minute meditation, done twice a day and designed to pause your chaos, centre your energy, and allow you to gain control over your thoughts by kick-starting and wrapping up your day in a relaxing way. A music link is supplied for you to stream the meditational music I created for this.

Daily Questions

This step is very quick; a chance to get to know yourself and be interactive with 7 questions. You must complete this before you put down the guide to begin your day.

Nightly Read [less than 7 minutes]

Just a short daily chapter to get your thoughts focused and to equip you with various tools to help improve your daily thoughts, increase the positive energy, and inner peace.

Daily Summary

This is your chance to express your daily experiences; things you noticed; things you achieved or perhaps could have dealt with better throughout your day. This is great for noticing your patterns and encouraging progress.

Evening Meditation - Music Supplied

https://lnk.to/learningenergy

Same as step 2, except this time it's to complete your day in the best and elevated mood, giving you the best chance at an even more relaxed tomorrow. It is vital to complete both meditations to receive the full potential of this guide

Thought of the Night to Focus on While Falling Asleep

A simple thought to help keep your mind calm and to prevent your thoughts from running in stressful circles while you're trying to sleep. You must constantly bring yourself back to this thought whenever your mind wanders until you drift to sleep.

DAY 1

MORNING READ:

What You Focus on Grows

Good morning gorgeous!

Let's start by noticing that if you're ever feeling anything less than great, the best chance you have to turn it around and improve your mood is first thing in the morning. It is very important for you to be mindful of your thoughts and what you put your focus on immediately after you wake up. The thing you need to understand is that everything is energy! One little change of mood is tiny and easy to control at first but can very quickly get stronger and harder to stop if not dealt with accordingly.

Put it this way. Let's imagine two ways a common experience can work out. Imagine you can't find your keys, and of course it can be frustrating especially if you are already late to leave the house. Once you recognize the frustration, you choose to stay calm and keep the grumpiness under control while you rush around the house until you finally find them. That was easy! You decide to be thankful that you found them and encourage yourself to feel accomplished and positive, almost laughing at yourself for leaving everything to the last minute but feeling confident that it always seems to work out - you expected good things! In this version of events, you knew the keys were not worth ruining your day over, so you simply didn't let them!

In the second scenario, you could lose your keys and immediately stress out, imagining how bad things could get if you're any later than you already are. You may start to panic. You rush around the house clumsily. You swear. You spill your coffee and then your top is stained but you don't have a clean one that matches your outfit. Then you're mad that the laundry isn't done and you're making a huge mess, throwing things out of the way until you finally find your keys exactly where you left them. You basically freaked out for no reason but now you're extra late and you're a mess to match! You are utterly pissed off now. Once you leave the house you find traffic on your way. You're furious that someone has driven in front of you, they've cut you off, or maybe you've missed the bus and somehow you're even mad at the traffic light for being red. Damn! The red light isn't even human; it didn't specifically select you as a target to ruin your day. But now you're in a bad 'mood' and you were distracted trying to find your keys earlier, so you forgot to text someone back that you were speaking to. Now you've received a text saying 'cool' or 'k then' because they're upset, thinking you're ignoring them. Things somehow keep getting worse in a ripple effect and it can immediately feel like the world is against you.

We all know a stress head like this second example. Being around them while they freak out is such an overwhelming energy to experience – and not a good type of overwhelming. When we allow ourselves to snowball into a highly anxious state of mind, we think that everything is falling apart but that isn't the case at all. All it was, was that little moment in the morning when you misplaced your keys; you didn't notice that negative emotion gaining momentum and getting stronger. Otherwise you would be able to make a prior deliberate and conscious decision to control your reaction and prevent it from impacting your day. Once something speeds up, it is harder to slow down. In this case, it was the lost keys. In the first way mentioned above, the stress was controlled. In other words, something that could have blown out of proportion was maintained. In the second outcome, the stress and anxiety were not controlled and quickly blew out of proportion. It will require some great energy to stop it now.

Imagine the stress of losing the keys in the example as being a big human sized basketball. If you're standing toward the top of a steep hill and someone standing a little further up the hill releases that huge basketball down towards you whilst you're standing a few feet away, you can stop it without much energy. You could put your arms out and stop it from rolling because you caught it early. You managed to notice it coming and you knew how to stop it. However, if you're standing at the bottom of the hill and someone pushes the large basketball down directly at you, what will happen if you try to suddenly stop it? The ball will gain lots of speed and become far more powerful - it will knock you right over and do some serious damage. Keep in mind the tiny push at the top of the hill wasn't any stronger either times the massive basketball was released. My point is, you have to catch your emotions as early as possible if you want a chance at improving them or preventing yourself from spiraling out of control.

So, here we go! Be mindful!

MORNING MEDITATION:

A Way to Clear Your Mind

It is now time to do a 7 minute meditation. For those who are experienced, you can get started as you already know the deal. For the beginners that are new to meditation, make sure to turn all electrical devices off or on silent then lay down on your back or sit upright in a comfortable position with your eyes closed for the entire duration of the music. It is important to find a relaxing position so you have the best chance at not shuffling and moving around during your meditation.

The goal is to have both your body and mind still. It may be a little unusual at first but you will notice the difference with ease by day 7.

You will naturally have thoughts pop into your mind but it is your duty to let them pass - watch them like clouds in the sky and don't focus on them. Do not give them power to start worrying you. In these short 7 minutes, you are allowed to let all your worries go; all your concerns and the things you have to get done are not welcome! Be still, breathe, and release your air deeply and slowly notice each muscle relax.

Please pull up the supplied audio and enjoy on all platforms! (See INDEX PAGE, page 134, TO LOCATE MUSIC)

Please sign below if you have completed the meditation exercise.

Signature: ……………………………

DAILY QUESTIONS

1. What are some of your qualities you're proud of?

   ....
   ....
   ....
   ....
   ....
   ....
   ....

2. Why are you proud of these qualities?

   ....
   ....
   ....
   ....
   ....

....

....

3. What would you say people like about you as a
   person?

   ....

   ....

   ....

   ....

   ....

   ....

   ....

4. What 3 things are you thankful for in your life
   right now? (Example, I am thankful that I have a
   bed to sleep in at night, or, I am thankful my
   friend saves me a seat in class, or I am thankful
   to have a sibling).

   ....

   ....

   ....

   ....

   ....

   ....

   ....

5. Why are you thankful for those 3 things?

....

....

....

....

....

....

....

6. What is one thing about yourself that you wish you could change?

....

....

....

....

....

....

....

7. Why do you think you'd be happier if it did change?

....

....

....

....

....

....

....

NIGHTLY READ:

Unlearning What You Have Been Taught

You have been programmed since you were born: by your family, siblings, movies, TV shows, songs, teachers, advertisements and more to lead you to believe a massive combination of 'facts' about who you are and what you should be. Obviously, we are eventually going to believe what people constantly say. That is all we know - and as young humans, we look for leadership and guidance with our pure souls and we believe the 'facts' we are told. We are told how to speak, how to think, what to wear, how to act, that we are too loud, that we eat too much, that we need to become this or that and we slowly absorb a huge load of opinions which our conscious and subconscious mind shifts through. Eventually, things stick.

We develop this idea of who we are, but that is just like reading a movie review from a brand new release you just watched and loved, yet someone wrote a review that you don't agree with at all!

Everyone's reality is different and all these ideas we convinced ourselves are 'facts' about who we are, are just opinions of others. These opinions are just are just projections that others have forced upon us in an attempt to deal with themselves. It is easier for someone to not hate themselves for never chasing their dreams of being an actor if they tell you you're crazy for wanting to be something just as challenging such as a movie producer, a singer, a dancer etc - it makes them feel better about their life decisions. People's opinions about you are always more about THEM than you.

We prevent ourselves from self reflecting because we believe what people say about us and we keep comparing ourselves to people online or on TV. We are always looking outside instead of within ourselves. The second you start to take accountability for yourself and the things you choose to believe in is when you start to see changes.

Whatever 'facts' you believe about yourself that are not uplifting, can be changed in your mind! Just like someone's review on a movie can change the second time around after watching or just like you can simply respect their review (saying a movie was terrible) and confidently know it was a great movie instead. You don't allow their review to impact your 'facts'.

Whether it be that you think you're too loud, too confronting, too fat, too skinny, too needy or irritating, all these 'facts' are changeable in your mind. No one's opinion can hurt us other than our own unless we allow it. We hold the power within ourselves to be happy and peaceful. We were all pure souls, nothing but love and light before coming into the world and being given a body for a short experience of life! We hold the key internally, to all power and happiness. The goal is to remember that and start working on ourselves from the inside out.

We slowly forget that as life happens, we tend to get confused because we are pulled in so many different directions. We develop a false idea about who we are with all these horrible 'flaws' and somehow believe that power and happiness come from other people's opinions. We think we will be happy if we find a relationship, get a new car, the perfect set of eyebrows, sculpted six-pack abs or find some popular friends. No matter what you achieve from your outside environment, you will never feel at peace if you are not at peace within.

We need to dig through all the lies, all the false 'facts', and all the opinions and remember who we are. We are good souls made of pure love - who just want to love and be loved. We just want to feel a sense of belonging in a world that is all about being connected with each other.

We are all one, we are all connected, and we are all capable of impacting anything and everything, even with a single thought. One single domino can be knocked over to hit another domino almost double its size. Then this domino will continue to fall and hit many others in line, continuing with enough momentum to push over much larger objects. This quickly growing power gradually gets bigger and bigger to generate enough force to move buses and buildings. That is basic science.

Just like a huge line of dominos and objects, the power of a single thought can change the world as it continues to grow and influence something else. You just need to decide which thoughts are constructive. You need to figure out which thoughts you should allow to grow and which thoughts do not deserve the momentum. So, who are you? It is time you realized that this is YOUR choice, not anyone else's. You get to decide what you think of yourself and you have the ability to control what you give power to!

DAILY SUMMARY:

A Moment of Self-reflection

Write below a collection of thoughts or experiences from today. It can involve triggers you noticed where your mood almost changed (or did change), what you're proud of, or how you could have handled it differently. Things you enjoyed about your day or things that may have not gone to plan. Monitor how you're currently reacting as well as how you would like to learn to react. This should just be a diary form entry for you to keep track of your habits, progress, or areas requiring some self-reflection. Let it all out!

....

....

....

....

....

....

....

....
....
....
....
....
....
....
....
....
....
....
....
....
....
....
....
....
....
....
....
....
....
....
....
....

....
....
....
....
....
....
....
....
....
....
....
....
....
....
....
....
....
....
....
....
....
....
....
....
....
....
....
....
....

....
....
....
....
....
....
....
....
....
....
....
....
....
....
....
....
....
....
....
....
....
....
....
....
....
....
....
....

EVENING MEDITATION:

(*You may wish to skip reading if you're already familiar with the instructions*)

This meditation exercise is the same as the morning meditation. Unless you're already familiar with the instructions, please refer to the morning meditation.

Please sign below if you have completed the meditation exercise.

Signature: ....

NIGHTLY THOUGHT

"I get to decide who I am and who I want to become. It is my choice."

DAY 2

MORNING READ:

Raising Your Vibration

Good morning gorgeous!

So, what is this 'vibrational' talk everyone goes on about when they're talking about good vibes, or mental health, or spirituality? Everything is energy and everything has its own vibrational frequency which can be high, low or anywhere in between. Better feeling emotions such as love, joy and happiness are considered to be 'high-vibrating' while the negative emotions such as sadness or hatred are lower and slower and don't feel as good.

The amazing thing about being human is we literally have our own in-built emotional GPS that warns and encourages us at times if we know how to understand what it is telling us through feeling. We can learn a lot about ourselves by listening to our feelings, which may at first not make sense.

Think about it. When things are working out for you, such as getting a call back from a job, an audition, or someone you have feelings for starts giving you attention back, what do you feel? You feel happy and hopeful! What happens in an opposite scenario occurs? Such as when you've fallen off your routine, when you aren't as productive as you planned to be that week, or when you hang around negative people who are distracting you from your goals? What do you feel? Your belly no longer feels hopeful and happy, that's for sure. You suddenly feel off, drained, concerned, or worried. These are low vibrations. The emotions you feel guide you towards thoughts, people, decisions and experiences of the same vibration - in other words, you attract what you feel. You attract the same vibrating experiences into your life. Your emotional GPS can help you discover what you want and what you don't want throughout your life if you learn to notice the shift in your emotions and to redirect your focus when needed.

Let's imagine you have a friend that tends to disappoint you or let you down at times. Your energy and intuition will often warn you far before anything gets sour that something is not right. If you focus on your emotional GPS, it will be a bunch of feelings in your belly that is sending you signals at all times! This can help you navigate away from what is weighing you down and give you the option to choose to redirect towards a routine that feels good. Changing your focus for the better results in raising your vibration and in turn attracts great things into your daily experience. In the case of having a 'friend' that doesn't quite add positive value to your life, your emotions will be shooting warnings of 'off' feelings, hoping you get the hint that perhaps you should distance yourself from them before things take a turn for the worse. You don't feel good when you are experiencing or thinking about things that are not in alignment with your true self. Your true self, is that soul part of you that is full of love. It is your pure self that existed before you were given a human body and a life on earth.

You are pure love, peace, and understanding. Every time something happens that is not vibrating at the same frequency as love, your emotional GPS starts to shoot out lower vibrating emotions that give us the chance to get back on track if we take notice. Everyone just wants to feel good! Make an effort to listen to and appreciate your emotions.

If you're anxious, respect that feeling and figure out what people, places, thoughts or experiences are triggering that lower vibration and try to change the uncomfortable causes. It may be as simple as redirecting a negative thought that you might have not noticed you think a lot about. Or it may be a friend you spend too much time around that isn't actually looking out for your best interest.

Perhaps it is your diet, your relationship or your workplace. Start to figure out the patterns of what triggers your lower vibrations that throw you to a negative state of being and have you stuck in a negative cycle. Do more of that feels good!

So let's recap. We must remember that in the morning, or at the moment you first wake up is the best opportunity to grab control of your energy and vibration. That is the best chance you get to direct your focus and begin to deliberately give momentum and strength to positive emotions and happier energy such as feeling hopeful, feeling calm, content or satisfied.

Remember the example of the large basketball not being able to roll over you if pushed downhill towards you from a short distance, yet knocking you right over once it speeds up? Let the good energy speed up and block the sad thoughts before they gain momentum and knock you over! Figure out what parts of your life influence good vibrations and which do not.

It is no one else's responsibility or business to do this for you. It might seem difficult at first but I promise it gets easier and easier until it is automatic for you to feel positive things for the majority of your day. If you work on this you will quickly notice when people or circumstances are threatening your energy and be about to protect your good vibes. Hopefully you slept well and you're reading this before you got up to check your phone or get distracted on the way to the bathroom haha!

MORNING MEDITATION:

A Way to Clear Your Mind

It is now time to do a 7 minute meditation. For those who are experienced, you can get started as you already know the deal. For the beginners that are new to meditation, make sure to turn all electrical devices off or on silent then lay down on your back or sit upright in a comfortable position with your eyes closed for the entire duration of the music. It is important to find a relaxing position so you have the best chance at not shuffling and moving around during your meditation.

The goal is to have both your body and mind still. It may be a little unusual at first but you will notice the difference with ease by day 7.

You will naturally have thoughts pop into your mind but it is your duty to let them pass - watch them like clouds in the sky and don't focus on them. Do not give them power to start worrying you. In these short 7 minutes, you are allowed to let all your worries go; all your concerns and the things you have to get done are not welcome! Be still, breathe, and release your air deeply and slowly notice each muscle relax.

Please pull up the supplied audio and enjoy on all platforms! (See INDEX PAGE, page 134, TO LOCATE MUSIC)

Please sign below if you have completed the meditation exercise.

Signature: ....

DAILY QUESTIONS

1. What thoughts have you noticed you often think that don't feel good?

....
....
....
....
....
....
....

2. Why do you think they don't feel good?

....
....
....
....
....
....
....

3. What do you think makes someone a good friend?

....
....
....
....
....
....
....

4. How do you like to be treated by your friends and family?

....
....
....
....
....
....
....

5. Do you treat your friends and family the way you explained above in question 4?

....
....
....
....
....
....
....

6. What are two ways you could improve as a friend, regardless of how people treat you?

....
....
....

....

....

....

....

7. Describe your perfect idea of a holiday or getaway from all responsibilities.

....

....

....

....

....

....

....

NIGHTLY READ:

Learning to Control Our Thoughts

I once met someone who told me to filter my thoughts *as if they were words coming out of the mouth of someone sitting next to me*. This didn't really make much sense until I went home and truly thought about what this meant. Then it clicked!

Why are we so allowing of these negative thoughts in our brains, hammering over and over again? If someone was sitting next to you, trying to get you worried saying, "Oh, you're going to be late, what are you doing? Helloooo, Stupid! You are late! Now you're later! What are you doing? You always do this! You're so unreliable. You're going to be late. You don't even look good, what are you wearing? Bet you can't find your keys," you'd walk away from that person. You simply wouldn't tolerate someone yelling unproductive things in your ear, however we allow our minds to say negative things all day long. Filter these thoughts this way: If you wouldn't want to hear someone saying it to you in person, don't allow yourself to continue thinking the thought. It is natural to question things we think but it is our choice to approve continuing to think the thoughts and to confirm whether we agree or not. We have the ability to continue or discontinue the focus and energy towards a thought.

I have read many books that explain this in their own way too, but the best way I can teach you is this: You are not your emotions just like you are not your thoughts. If you can see the TV in front of you and hear the birds chirping outside, understand that you are neither the TV nor the birds. You are the one that is observing those exterior objects and if you can hear the thoughts, then you are not the thoughts you think.

YOU are much deeper than the thoughts YOU think - YOU hear things, YOU see things just like YOU touch and taste. So you are neither these emotions nor the thoughts so toughen up and take control of them.

Whenever anyone does anything in life, they are always doing it with the intention of feeling good. Even if someone is doing something disastrous they still have it in their mind that they will feel good after doing it. At our very core, we are all a ball of goodness, with good intention and a hunger to live. We want to experience as much as we can in this one lifetime and we can use our thoughts to our advantage or allow them to be a disadvantage.

Your emotions are a language used by your human body to speak to your inner-self about how in tune or out of tune you are with your true frequency. The more we do that is in line with our natural loving selves at our core, the better we feel and the higher our vibration is. If someone puts you down, it will hurt you and you will feel emotions of sadness. This is because they have pulled you away from the vibration of who you really are - they pulled you away from love. In these moments, our emotional GPS will alarm us that we are being distracted. It is up to us to change our focus and to control our thoughts before they gain momentum and lower our energy. If you can control your thoughts then your thoughts shouldn't control you!

Your honest and inner-self is kind, understanding, peaceful and joyous. The more you are able to speak, think, eat, talk, love, act, and live in the rhythm that match that deep inner buzz inside of you, the happier you will be in life even when alone at home. As I mentioned before, you will also attract what you feel in life. Everything in the world has its own frequency or vibration and you will run into more people and experiences that match with how you're feeling. So be in control of that!

Trust your emotions as they guide you through life. When you discover moments of negativity, you will begin to notice the vibrational change - this is your little red flag waving inside trying to help you take a step in a new direction before you spiral out of control. Learn to understand your emotional language, your internal GPS, and you will control what thoughts feel good and which ones you should dismiss. Use your emotional GPS to decide which thoughts you impact you and which you will not.

DAILY SUMMARY:

A Moment of Self-reflection

Write below a collection of thoughts or experiences from today. It can involve triggers you noticed where your mood almost changed (or did change), what you're proud of, or how you could have handled it differently. Things you enjoyed about your day or things that may have not gone to plan. Monitor how you're currently reacting as well as how you would like to learn to react. This should just be a diary form entry for you to keep track of your habits, progress, or areas requiring some self-reflection. Let it all out!

....
....
....
....
....
....
....
....
....
....
....

....
....
....
....
....
....
....
....
....
....
....
....
....
....
....
....
....
....
....
....
....
....
....
....
....

EVENING MEDITATION:

A Way to Clear Your Mind

(*You may wish to skip reading if you're already familiar with the instructions*)

This meditation exercise is the same as the morning meditation. Unless you're already familiar with the instructions, please refer to the morning meditation.

Please sign below if you have completed the meditation exercise.

Signature: ....

NIGHTLY THOUGHT

"I am in control of my thoughts! I will do my

best to be selective with which thoughts I

welcome and which I dismiss."

Optional Activity 1

(Colour me in)

DAY 3

MORNING READ:

Law of Attraction

Top of the morning sweetheart!

This next chapter is important. I'm sure you have heard of the 'law of attraction' and also been told about the importance of affirmations. If you haven't, most general definitions will describe the 'Law of Attraction' as something along the lines of "whatever you focus on and desire will be attracted into your life."

On the other hand, affirmations are simply a bunch of confirmations you 'affirm' or tell yourself such as, "I am beautiful" or "I am strong." I am a firm believer in the use of both of these concepts, however in my opinion there is something that is often left out of these teachings.

The world is all energy and you attract more of what you feel rather than what you say. While words certainly have power and carry weight, it is more so the feeling behind those words that can influence energy.

This applies to both the 'Law of Attraction' and using affirmations to improve your quality of life. Think of it this way. If you're feeling down, it often isn't the best idea to say, "I am happy" over and over again in the mirror, attempting to say an affirmation and attract happiness into your life as some self-help books suggest. All that happens is you're indirectly emphasizing your lack of feeling happy and highlighting the fact you're sad. You are giving unintentional energy and focus towards your negative vibration where you lack happiness. You're often just confirming to yourself, "I am unhappy".

When it comes to attracting things into your life, the most productive and successful experiences I have personally had and read from others, come from visualization of your desire matched with the feeling that you would have if you were to achieve or gain this desire. In other words, if you are dreaming of finding a romantic partner, you're more likely to manifest that by envisioning it in your imagination and also finding a feeling of joy, safety and excitement that you would expect to feel if you found them. You can achieve this by memorizing moments in life when you felt similar emotions. Life may not be the way at the moment but you can still tap into those memories and generate a similar buzz in your belly. You need to feel the way you would hope to feel and you will attract it. I know it will seem impossible to feel happy but you can tap into these energies from the past. Think of a birthday, a holiday, winning a soccer game, receiving a prize, a gift - tap into whatever memory you can that may bring you closest to how you would feel when achieving your goals into your life!

If these memories don't get you entirely happy or excited in that moment, you at least can FEEL a little better whilst trying to manifest something or whilst saying affirmations. Once you get to that place emotionally, focus on the fact you're feeling better and that already is a step closer to matching the energy of your goals. If you want to attract your dream house, car or job then you should imagine having it in your brain and do all you can to create the emotions you would feel if you had these things. If you can imagine the feeling of how great life would be to have these desires, then you can influence your present vibration to match the vibration of what you desire.

The universe will listen to how you feel! You will attract what you feel!

MORNING MEDITATION:

A Way to Clear Your Mind

It is now time to do a 7 minute meditation. For those who are experienced, you can get started as you already know the deal. For the beginners that are new to meditation, make sure to turn all electrical devices off or on silent then lay down on your back or sit upright in a comfortable position with your eyes closed for the entire duration of the music. It is important to find a relaxing position so you have the best chance at not shuffling and moving around during your meditation.

The goal is to have both your body and mind still. It may be a little unusual at first but you will notice the difference with ease by day 7.

You will naturally have thoughts pop into your mind but it is your duty to let them pass - watch them like clouds in the sky and don't focus on them. Do not give them power to start worrying you. In these short 7 minutes, you are allowed to let all your worries go; all your concerns and the things you have to get done are not welcome! Be still, breathe, and release your air deeply and slowly notice each muscle relax.

Please pull up the supplied audio and enjoy on all platforms! (See INDEX PAGE, page 134, TO LOCATE MUSIC)

Please sign below if you have completed the meditation exercise.

Signature: ....

DAILY QUESTIONS

1. How did you feel when you first woke up this morning?

   ....

   ....

   ....

   ....

   ....

   ....

   ....

2. What did you like about your day today?

   ....

   ....

   ....

   ....

....

....

....

3. How much do you care about what other people care about you?

....

....

....

....

....

....

....

4. If you were to fail at something, are you the type to try again or give up?

....

....

....

....

....

....

....

5. Why do you think you're that way?

....
....
....
....
....
....
....

6. What do you want to get out of life?

....
....
....
....
....
....
....

7. If you could achieve anything right now, what would it be?

....
....
....
....
....
....
....

NIGHTLY READ:

Your True Potential Will Unlock When You Defy Comfort

Good evening honey, hope you have had a good day so far. I want to take a second to speak to you about your current position in life. We need to stop accepting what we do not want! Are you happy with your life? Your daily motivation?Productivity?Income? Are you happy with how active you are, or have you travelled to your dream destinations yet? The point I am coming to is, we need to stop tolerating our current circumstances.

We continue to experience what we tolerate. If you want to see a change in anything, you need to first be that change youreslf - do the initial internal job of personal development. Stop sending signals out to the universe that you accept your current lifestyle. Stop accepting the way things are and repeating your weekly habits, having pointless conversations, watching too much TV or simply not actively working towards any sort of goal or achievement.

You are amazing, you're great! The fact you're reading this book tells me that you know there is more to life and more that you can offer. Do not allow yourself to settle in any way - shape or form. You become a byproduct of the people you hang around, the things you listen to, the thoughts you think, the programs you watch on TV and so forth. Don't be afraid to switch it up! Stop focusing on the reasons why you cannot change someone, leave something or try something new and only allow yourself to focus on one reason as to why you can!

Most new things in life are scary; they are new and unfamiliar. It may be a new school, a new yoga class, an online course, a solo trip overseas, or applying for medicine school after your 50's - but if you aren't going to do it for yourself, no one will! The most amazing things are waiting for you on the other side of fear and concern and you can change this by first deciding to no longer tolerate your current situation in life. Push the boundaries!

I look back and I'm deeply thankful for the times I somehow found the courage to try something new, even when it meant possibly looking stupid, losing friends, missing out on special occasions or simply going against what everyone advised me. I am grateful every day for the times I failed when I took the leap because every "NO", or every time I fell short of success, still took me a step closer to a "YES"! It also took me a step closer to the person I am today. I am so happy I didn't take the safer roads in life.

Whatever it is that you have had lying in the back of your mind, or whatever it is that you have watched someone achieve online, you can do it!

DAILY SUMMARY:

A Moment of Self-reflection

Write below a collection of thoughts or experiences from today. It can involve triggers you noticed where your mood almost changed (or did change), what you're proud of, or how you could have handled it differently. Things you enjoyed about your day or things that may have not gone to plan. Monitor how you're currently reacting as well as how you would like to learn to react. This should just be a diary form entry for you to keep track of your habits, progress, or areas requiring some self-reflection. Let it all out!

....

....

....

....

....
....
....
....
....
....
....
....
....
....
....
....
....
....
....
....
....
....
....
....
....
....
....
....
....

....
....
....
....
....
....
....
....
....
....
....
....
....
....
....
....
....
....
....
....
....
....
....
....
....
....
....
....

EVENING MEDITATION:

A Way to Clear Your Mind

(*You may wish to skip reading if you're already familiar with the instructions*)

This meditation exercise is the same as the morning meditation. Unless you're already familiar with the instructions, please refer to the morning meditation.

Please sign below if you have completed the meditation exercise.

Signature: ……………………………

NIGHTLY THOUGHT

"I get to choose what I continue to accept in my life! What I allow will continue."

DAY 4

MORNING READ:

How to Transition into Feeling Positive

Most people have a great intention of trying to begin feeling happy but they're aiming for such a high-vibrational energy from an extremely low-vibrational place such as depression or guilt. While this is a good intention, what they often fail to realize is that it is much more likely to reach happiness if you work your way towards that emotional direction - bouncing along more accessible vibrations along the way.

This might sound crazy but it is much better to feel angry or enraged than it is to feel depressed as these emotional states are all 'neighbours' vibrationally. This is because depression is the darkest and most powerless emotion. To be angry, is a fraction closer to happiness than depression because you gain some power back unlike being depressed and powerless. To be angry is to have power - even if it isn't felt in the sweetest way.

Anger is a closer vibration to depression than it is to happiness, so anger is an easier emotion to access when you're depressed.

Lots of people will continuously let themselves down when they're trying to get out of a rut and this can be tiring! I get it, you've tried and tried and all you do is fail to feel any better, causing you to feel worse. Sometimes it can feel as though if you see just one more positive quote on Instagram you're going to lose your mind!

If you're feeling anything less than great, or know someone who is, you should really soak up this tool. Even the slightest improvement with your mood can be the most amazing victory when you've been stuck feeling heavy, alone, and down for a while. A tiny improvement could be all you need to start to feel like yourself again, giving you the ability to gain momentum back toward a happy place, bouncing along emotions that aren't so far away from your current feeling. So how do we do it?

First, acknowledge the place you're at vibrationally and emotionally. Make it your goal to tap into the next best emotion because it is far more accessible than aiming too far away! If you're feeling insecure, this energy somewhat matches the energy of hopefulness.

While being hopeful doesn't feel like the most exciting achievement to aim for, it is a step up the scale towards happiness but first is closer to a neutral vibration of feeling contempt. Once you get to a place over the next few days where you've tapped into feeling hopeful and then perhaps contempt, you then have an easier pass to shifting your vibration into an emotion of acceptance. When you're feeling acceptance, you can work toward a feeling of eagerness, then forgiveness, then trust and finally feel confident. It is far more incredible to feel confident rather than insecure yet if you tried to jump from insecure to confident overnight, you're likely to miss and end up frustrated; potentially feeling even lower than feeling insecure in the first place.

My point is, all emotions are vibrations and if we ever find ourselves in the lower range and want a safe and progressive way out, it is often wise to work your way up the scale rather than take a risky leap! Take a look at this diagram to better understand.

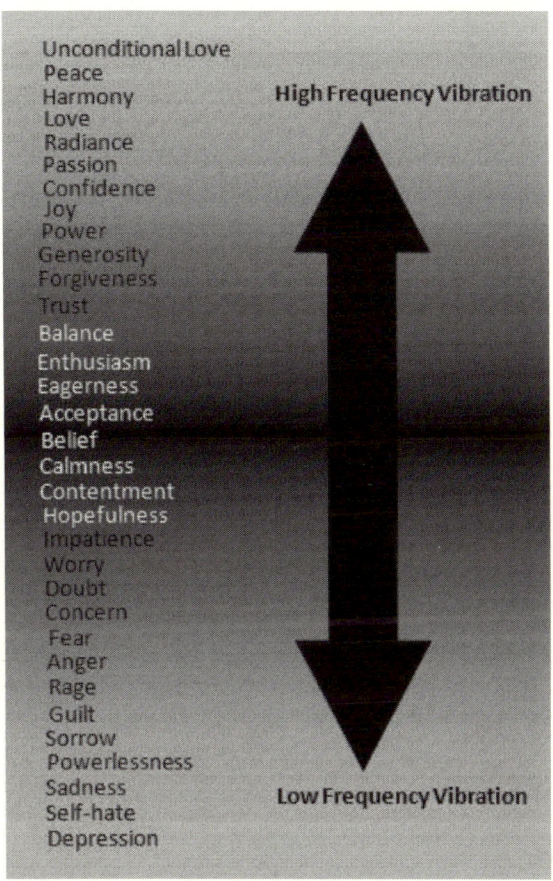

(List of Emotions)

MORNING MEDITATION:

A Way to Clear Your Mind

It is now time to do a 7 minute meditation. For those who are experienced, you can get started as you already know the deal. For the beginners that are new to meditation, make sure to turn all electrical devices off or on silent then lay down on your back or sit upright in a comfortable position with your eyes closed for the entire duration of the music. It is important to find a relaxing position so you have the best chance at not shuffling and moving around during your meditation.

The goal is to have both your body and mind still. It may be a little unusual at first but you will notice the difference with ease by day 7.

You will naturally have thoughts pop into your mind but it is your duty to let them pass - watch them like clouds in the sky and don't focus on them. Do not give them power to start worrying you. In these short 7 minutes, you are allowed to let all your worries go; all your concerns and the things you have to get done are not welcome! Be still, breathe, and release your air deeply and slowly notice each muscle relax.

Please pull up the supplied audio and enjoy on all platforms! (See INDEX PAGE, page 134, TO LOCATE MUSIC)

Please sign below if you have completed the meditation exercise.

Signature: ....

DAILY QUESTIONS

Word Search

```
P U S I L D C T U C Z S I P R
H E X A O N C P Q O H P V O T
T O S F V S P U V N Y A I W D
R T N N E C U R T S I T D A P
Q X E E K T T I D I J I Z O S
Q L J M S D N T O D P E Q B O
E Y O G R T A Y N E I N N E O
E M T Y N U Y O R R T C R L M
Q U P X A R M E O A R E E I N
H B G A C L V P A T U B S E Z
E L W U T E T Y Q I S C P F J
F L F F Y H U Y I O T B E P V
W Z S W T R Y C X N K U C X G
W C D M N G C R B H T K T V P
E W W Z M T I E C V Y R R F F
```

consideration	patience	empathy	honesty
loyalty	respect	purity	belief
trust	love		

(Diagram of find a word)

1. Circle the first 4 words you see in the diagram above.

2. Do you think you use your time wisely? Justify your answer.

    a) Yes

    b) No

....
....
....
....
....
....
....

3. Do you think you exercise enough to consider yourself in healthy shape and how could you take your physical health to the next level?

....
....
....
....
....
....
....

4. Are you proud of who you are?

....
....
....
....
....

....

....

5. What is one of your happy childhood
    memories?

    ....

    ....

    ....

    ....

    ....

    ....

    ....

6. Who impacts your life that you do not
    personally know?

    ....

    ....

    ....

    ....

    ....

    ....

    ....

    ....

    ....

    ....

7. If you could take any of that person's characteristics and make them yours, which would they be?

....
....
....
....
....
....
....

NIGHTLY READ:

Bargaining with Life on Your Own Terms

When we were young, most of us have had parents or guardians who did their best in raising us. You could have been raised by your grandpa, grandma, your sister, your neighbour or a stranger that became part of your life. Based on their upbringing, culture and life experiences, they did the best they could to teach us wrong from right through their own eyes in a society that directly and indirectly told us who we should and shouldn't be in life.

Something you realize as you grow up is our parents are also just giant kids trying to figure this journey out too. No one is perfect and no one was given the correct to-do list to get it absolutely right.

Isn't it weird that when you're young, the general idea is that parents have it all figured out and that adults never really get it wrong in life? However, we soon learn that we had that perception massively mixed up. In fact, it is amazing how much you can observe and learn from the opposite of a parent - a baby, or a young child! They are pure little souls, experiencing life with less pressure regarding who they should be and how they should act and this purity is so calming to observe. Babies do what they like; they're excited, they want to taste and touch everything and simply explore their surroundings. They are always giggling, burping, vomiting, and farting with no shame along the way. Babies are pure and curious, and we often lose those traits along with our ability to live an unfiltered life as we grow up. They just want to eat, sleep and feel comfortable. As long as they feel loved and protected, they naturally let off so much love and security in return. You can feel the love from an infant even if you're a stranger that catches eye contact and notices a little smile. We need to be more like our baby selves!

A lot of my spiritual journey was about unlearning things that were programmed into me by people who thought they knew what was best for me. Adults try to protect you from making the same mistakes they did. They often try to prevent you from being hurt and often stop you from making them question their own paths in their own life. Your parents may have a way of life, a list of rules, a perception of what is acceptable and what isn't that you may disagree with. Maybe the majority of what you don't agree with has to do with maturity and your opinion will change when you're older. Maybe you will agree with them when you have bills or if you become a parent one day. But maybe you don't agree because times have changed or you don't want to live life by the same book, by the same standard or by the same limitations. This is for you to decide. Do not be afraid to observe and question why you don't feel at ease with many rules and the pressure placed upon you.

If I followed society's expectations of me, along with my parents' influence, I would have focused a lot more on my studies and less on creating music. I chose to focus on a boy who distracted me but gave me the experience to write songs that got me noticed to start a music career. I instead would have left high school and went straight to university. I would have stayed in university even though I hated it and I would have been saving money and owned a few properties by now. Both lives would have probably been great but they are completely different realities in the end. Which reality do you want?

Yes, I'd be 'successful' through society's eyes. Instead, I was a little louder than society wanted me to be and tended to often challenge expectations. I don't want to sound like I am encouraging everyone to be a rebel, break the rules and push back the advice of their loved ones. However don't be so quick to ignore the fire in your belly to be different as long as it is not malicious or illegal, haha!

If I did as the world suggested, I wouldn't have moved overseas, I wouldn't have started and quit over 30 jobs which was what enabled me to discover that I wanted to work for myself. I would not have switched university degrees 3 times and still decided it wasn't for me because that seems careless. I wouldn't have made it onto the music charts and gained over 150 million streams or performed live in front of millions around the world. I wouldn't be waking up and paying my bills by doing what I love to do!

Being a success means something different to each person and it is up to you to figure out what that is. Success is relative. You can spend your life pleasing others but are they spending their life pleasing you?

One thing I know for sure is that if I didn't try, I would be miserable even with a double bachelor degree, a few properties in my name and lots of money in the bank. Right now, I am in a different phase of life, and my idea of success is evolving as I have checked certain things off my life's goal-list. I realize a lot of parents mean well, but are only teaching their children within the limitations of their own experiences. They are only trying to protect them.

Lots of our elders didn't get to chase their dreams, or didn't have google or fast-paced technological tools to self-educate, to make a plan to create a business or study online. They focused on survival. My point is, people can mean well but still, unintentionally, hold you back. Often people will not agree at first but once you persist, they will be glad and happy for you finding yourself even if it is off the typical grid and even if you paved a new path brand new to their experiences. Everyone ends up supporting you once you prove yourself, you just need to be your own cheerleader even when no one else quite sees your vision.

DAILY SUMMARY:

A Moment of Self-reflection

Write below a collection of thoughts or experiences from today. It can involve triggers you noticed where your mood almost changed (or did change), what you're proud of, or how you could have handled it differently. Things you enjoyed about your day or things that may have not gone to plan. Monitor how you're currently reacting as well as how you would like to learn to react. This should just be a diary form entry for you to keep track of your habits, progress, or areas requiring some self-reflection. Let it all out!

....

....

....

....

....

....

....

....

....

....

....

....
....
....
....
....
....
....
....
....
....
....
....
....
....
....
....
....
....
....
....
....
....
....
....

....
....
....
....
....
....
....
....
....
....
....
....
....
....
....
....
....
....
....
....
....
....
....
....
....
....
....
....

EVENING MEDITATION:

A Way to Clear Your Mind

(*You may wish to skip reading if you're already familiar with the instructions*)

This meditation exercise is the same as the morning meditation. Unless you're already familiar with the instructions, please refer to the morning meditation.

Please sign below if you have completed the meditation exercise.

Signature: ....

NIGHTLY THOUGHT

"We are all here to learn and unlearn our way through life; everyone is a student."

<u>Optional Activity 2</u>

(Colour me in)

DAY 5

MORNING READ:
Taking Full Accountability

Good morning gorgeous, rise and shine!

I want to wake you up with an instant focus on self-awareness and self-accountability. Too many people are focused on the reasons why they cannot do something or why things cannot change. Too often than not, people use the excuse that they don't have the time to do what they claim they want to do when in fact they have the same daily 24 hours as every other human that exists in this world. So many of us are stuck in a self-limiting mindset.

It makes us feel better to accept that we are not where we would like to be with our relationships, finances or livelihood when we allow ourselves to believe we have no other choice. It takes courage to self-reflect and admit to yourself that the only person standing between you and your goals is YOU alongside your excuses! If you compare two people that are in the same field of work: Two Barbers for example cutting hair for 5 years - why might one excel into being their own boss and open up multiple store locations with 10 employees while the other still works at the same job yet struggles to get a pay rise from their boss? While education, talent, and resources may give someone an advantage over the other, someone with a vision, a plan, and a resilient attitude almost always can catch up if not overtake the other talented person despite them having an advantage.

We need to stop blaming others or blaming our current responsibilities as to why we are not growing. Focus on solutions and discover a way around current obstacles. Focus on the little things and big things can change: For example, you can sacrifice 30 minutes a day towards researching that new business you want to open; the workout you claim you don't have time to do, or to start working on your skills. You may not think you can but everyone has 30 minutes that they can immediately dedicate elsewhere that you currently spend on social media, texting, lying in bed, showering for longer than needed or procrastinating.

If you have something you wish you could do, somewhere you wish you could go, someone you wish you could meet or break up with, then you need to stop focusing on reasons why you cannot achieve this and only focus on the reasons why you can.

Make it your decision to focus on ways you can move towards change and growth. I used to blame record labels and point the finger at the dishonest nature of the music business as to why my music career hadn't 'blown up.' I had an excuse for everything and while lots of my points were true i.e. record labels just want to make money off you and producers try to hit on me because they are all male. I also don't make side money like everyone else because I am in America on a visa and I am not allowed to get any other job outside of my approval for generating money as a musician. I can't afford the budget for music videos, I don't buy social media followers and don't fake it like other people - clearly I had endless excuses involving people wanting to change me into an artist that I am not etc. These were true facts but they weren't reasons why I wasn't growing. They were just truths that I let control my potential to grow. Nothing has changed about those truths since I used to think like that, however I am now gaining hundreds of millions of streams and my music has made me hundreds of thousands of dollars. But how?

I stopped letting these things limit my potential. I stopped trying to make myself feel better - feeding into excuses and stopped using cover-up reasons - and put all that energy into focusing on being productive. I stopped relying on other people and started educating myself. I stopped using the excuse that I didn't have the time and I made the time. I stopped gossiping and dwelling on the same issues whenever I was let down and that seriously changed my life! I just kept it moving! I made to-do lists, a plan, and I stuck to them as best as I could. When I fell off, I got back on track as soon as I could and stopped wasting time being mad when people slowed me down.

I can assure you, there is someone in a far more challenging situation than you, perhaps with less access to information, money, in more debt, maybe with kids that they need to provide for that still is doing more than you to work toward a goal. There are people who are far less educated or that have some sort of physical or mental disability yet still have found a way to push through and achieve a goal. We need to take accountability for our lives even if there is someone limiting our resources or holding us back. It could be a family member, friend, or even colleague. If you focus on solutions, you WILL find them.

You need to find a way - with each attempt that doesn't work, you will be a step closer to finding a way that will. With every setback, you will learn something valuable. I am now a recording artist, signing other artists, songwriters and producers. I have my own recording studio and record label. I used to get rejected by every producer when I reached out to work together, or not be able to afford studio time. I was even rejected by the school choir for goodness' sake! I would not have the knowledge and the success I do today if I didn't experience those setbacks and I was the least likely in my primary school that you would guess who make a career out of music. If people didn't let me down, lie, steal my content or prevent me from having a chance then I wouldn't have worked so hard on my skills. So, wake up gorgeous! If I waited for the perfect moment, or for when I felt ready, or for when I had the time, I never would have done it!

Think about the things you wish you could do in your life and start focusing only on the possibilities.

Even if it seems impossible, it is possible!

MORNING MEDITATION:

A Way to Clear Your Mind

It is now time to do a 7 minute meditation. For those who are experienced, you can get started as you already know the deal. For the beginners that are new to meditation, make sure to turn all electrical devices off or on silent then lay down on your back or sit upright in a comfortable position with your eyes closed for the entire duration of the music. It is important to find a relaxing position so you have the best chance at not shuffling and moving around during your meditation.

The goal is to have both your body and mind still. It may be a little unusual at first but you will notice the difference with ease by day 7.

You will naturally have thoughts pop into your mind but it is your duty to let them pass - watch them like clouds in the sky and don't focus on them. Do not give them power to start worrying you. In these short 7 minutes, you are allowed to let all your worries go; all your concerns and the things you have to get done are not welcome! Be still, breathe, and release your air deeply and slowly notice each muscle relax.

Please pull up the supplied audio and enjoy on all platforms! (See INDEX PAGE, page 134, TO LOCATE MUSIC)

Please sign below if you have completed the meditation exercise.

Signature: ....

DAILY QUESTIONS

1. What are the 2 things that make you happy?

....

....

....

....

....

....

....

2. Give yourself 3 compliments:

....

....

....

....

....

....

....

3. When was the last time you attempted to get out
   of your comfort zone?

....

....

....

....

....

....

....

4. What worries you about the future?

....

....

....

....

....

....

....

5. What career would you have if you could have
   any?

....

....

....
....
....
....
....

6. What is your favourite hobby?

....
....
....
....
....
....
....

7. Why do you love it so much?

....
....
....
....
....
....
....
....
....
....

NIGHTLY READ:

Making a Shift in Focus

Welcome back! I hope you had a blessed day and didn't lose your mind. It is easy to get distracted by the chaos or irritated by daily duties and other people. It is up to us to centre ourselves and come back to an inner focus and alignment. It is one thing to meditate, to read something really useful that makes you feel better or to unwind and walk on the beach or amongst nature, however it is another thing to make it a habit and maintain those good emotions.

We find ways to destress and start to feel better but then we sometimes forget that this improvement in vibration isn't permanent without regular work. Don't hesitate to reread this guide once a month, or to make it a priority in your life to repeat whatever it is that may have helped you feel balanced. Let's just say reading really does help you align yourself and perhaps assists you in falling asleep quicker at night. Make an effort to introduce reading into your night every day, or perhaps once a week. We need to turn the tasks that feel good, into habits and routines in our life. If working out helps you feel good about yourself, then don't just hit the gym hard for a month and then fall off once you feel a little better about yourself. Make it a point to continue to go! Everyone responds differently to everything, so it is up to you to see what feels good, what encourages you to be more productive, who motivates you, or what slows you down. Make it an effort to notice how you respond. Then make a routine of it.

For me, I am the happiest when I don't stay up ridiculously late at night. This is because when my sleeping patterns are off - I tend to sleep in, then I feel mad at myself that I missed the morning. I then feel unproductive and blame the people that kept me awake. It is a domino effect.

I feel the best when I have a good sleeping pattern, when I drink lots of water a day, when I work out 3-4 times a week, when I read each night, when I follow some sort of healthy dietary guideline like drinking green juice or eating green veggies each day and when I follow a to-do list that I update every day. I feel better when I write things down and get them out of my head. I now notice straight away when these things shift because I feel, the emotions lowering.

I noticed when I let my emotions fall to lower vibrations that it continues to get worse unless I stop it. I used to have some days when I would think I'm near depressed but I would stay in control and get to the park for a walk instead of sitting on my phone avoiding the world. Then suddenly I bounce right back into my usual self! I thought I was depressed when really I just needed to get my blood circulating and change my focus. It's all about understanding yourself, seeing what works and what doesn't and holding yourself responsible to make certain things habits. We need to hand-select what we put our time into and our focus on. We need to be in control of what we give energy and momentum to. Attaining and maintaining inner peace takes daily work.

Your perception of the world around you is always based on what you're feeling inside. You are an amazing human being with a sweet soul. You deserve nothing but to feel happy, free, motivated, and elevated each day. You should be vibrating and smiling even when life challenges you. You have the ability to get to this state of being - it takes focus and discipline but it feels so good once you do it!

How good would it be to always be calm and trusting in your week ahead? How amazing would it feel to be working towards your goals and seeing progress every week? How amazing would it be, when the people around you start saying you look different, simply because your mindset has changed and you're glowing, letting off the best energy that even those who are not spiritual start to sense when they're around you? You can get there!

You are amazing and you should feel a little buzz of excitement in your belly right now because things truly will start to get better for you very quickly now that you are being reminded of all these tools. Have an amazing sleep, see you tomorrow!

DAILY SUMMARY:

A Moment of Self-reflection

Write below a collection of thoughts or experiences from today. It can involve triggers you noticed where your mood almost changed (or did change), what you're proud of, or how you could have handled it differently. Things you enjoyed about your day or things that may have not gone to plan. Monitor how you're currently reacting as well as how you would like to learn to react. This should just be a diary form entry for you to keep track of your habits, progress, or areas requiring some self-reflection. Let it all out!

....

....

....

....

....

....

....

....

....

....

....

....

....

....

....

....

....

....

....

....

....

....

....

....

....

....
....
....
....
....
....
....
....
....
....
....
....
....
....
....
....
....
....
....
....
....
....
....
....
....
....
....

....
....
....
....
....
....
....
....
....
....
....
....
....
....
....
....
....
....
....
....
....
....
....
....
....
....
....

EVENING MEDITATION:

A Way to Clear Your Mind

(*You may wish to skip reading if you're already familiar with the instructions*)

This meditation exercise is the same as the morning meditation. Unless you're already familiar with the instructions, please refer to the morning meditation.

Please sign below if you have completed the meditation exercise.

Signature: ……………………………

NIGHTLY THOUGHT

"I am excited to take control of my life and to spend more time doing things that make me feel good."

DAY 6

MORNING READ:

The Power of Restraint on Ego

Good morning, good morning!

I hope your sleep was a solid one. I want to spend a second to bring awareness to the simple fact that we have no idea what other people are going through. I know it's common to be served in a restaurant by a rude waiter and want to comment on how much of a cow or (your choice of insult) she is with her bad energy but we must make an effort to first pause.

In our daily lives, it is very common for us to be irritated by others once we lose a little control over our own vibration. Honestly, I don't always have everything figured out, I don't always follow my own advice and we all will occasionally 'fall off' on our shitty days even when we have our minds figured out. In the moments we judge others and are easily annoyed by some people's actions, the goal is to stay in control. If you have self control over your own vibration then you can experience people doing annoying or rude things and be unaffected. You can take note of when your peace is being threatened before you lose control. I'll be honest. I am still working on this myself as sometimes, I am inconsiderate. An experience I had lately involved signing into a boat club venue to have a surprise lunch for my cousin in Sydney. I was following the prompts on a touch-screen when the receptionist fiercely asked if I had a driver's license. I felt her energy like a cold shiver down my spine and looked up as she continued to snarl with a rushed and impatient energy, "You don't need to do that, just give me your license!"

I handed her my license for identification and let her know by my very obvious (wtf is wrong with you face) that I did not appreciate the way she was communicating. I overheard the end of her conversation with a couple next to me that she was also checking in. They had asked a question and she let them know they had to wait for her attention as she was busy with reports and turned her back before they had even ended eye contact with her. I don't know if they were friends of hers but when I saw her have that tension towards my sister too, I suddenly got defensive and asked her straight up, "Are you okay?" However, I didn't ask it with a genuine tone with the kind of intent I usually do, I asked it in a 'warning' type of way, insinuating I wasn't going to tolerate her attitude. She snapped back with a defensive face, "Why do you ask?" I told her, "I don't know, you just seem a little…eh." She barked back with a little attitude while forcing herself to remain somewhat professional behind her desk, "I'm finishing my reports!"

I took my license from her and decided to walk off. Even though I already had partially failed at being the calm and loving person I should have been, I knew I had a choice to continue to verbally challenge the woman and trust me, I can be a crazy bitch, or, I could leave it there as I really had no idea what the lady could be dealing with personally at that time in her life.

I continued with my lunch, held my cousin's new born baby and started answering my family's questions about my progress in Los Angeles. Suddenly the same lady walked up to our table with a completely different vibrational energy. She was on edge like a shy little girl, holding herself back from tears kneeled down by my table on the corner where I sat looking up at me, trying to not disturb everyone else's conversations. She apologized saying, "I'm so sorry if I came across the wrong way, I made a huge life decision last night and I am just really struggling." She broke my damn heart! I felt like such a monster but was so thankful I didn't flip out on her like I could have. I obviously knew she was miserable at the check in but my first defensive thought was, well yeah mate, shit isn't going great for me either right now but I'm not taking my stress out on you, woman! But after her apology, I really felt empathetic. Only God knows what the poor lady was going through or what she had gone through in the past, making her the way she was that day.

I could have genuinely asked her if she was okay instead of needing to feed my ego and put her in her place. My defensiveness spoke more poorly about myself than her. The same goes for when you have someone not moving in the car in front of you at the traffic-lights when it turns green, or when your teacher snaps at you for nothing at all, or your mother yells at you to do something without asking you kindly. You simply do not know what anyone is going through or what they have gone through in the past, making them the way they are today.

We are all on this journey in life and just a few words may be enough to push someone over the edge for good, or perhaps may be enough to impact their entire day for the better! I try my best to smile at most people, to say hello to the old man at the bus stop, or to compliment the shy girl on the train that is lowering her head showing signs of insecurity.

In conclusion, before you react to a situation, always try to keep in mind that you never know what someone is going through and you have the power to add to the negativity or to try to defuse it.

MORNING MEDITATION:

A Way to Clear Your Mind

It is now time to do a 7 minute meditation. For those who are experienced, you can get started as you already know the deal. For the beginners that are new to meditation, make sure to turn all electrical devices off or on silent then lay down on your back or sit upright in a comfortable position with your eyes closed for the entire duration of the music. It is important to find a relaxing position so you have the best chance at not shuffling and moving around during your meditation.

The goal is to have both your body and mind still. It may be a little unusual at first but you will notice the difference with ease by day 7.

You will naturally have thoughts pop into your mind but it is your duty to let them pass - watch them like clouds in the sky and don't focus on them. Do not give them power to start worrying you. In these short 7 minutes, you are allowed to let all your worries go; all your concerns and the things you have to get done are not welcome! Be still, breathe, and release your air deeply and slowly notice each muscle relax.

Please pull up the supplied audio and enjoy on all platforms! (See INDEX PAGE, page 134, TO LOCATE MUSIC)

Please sign below if you have completed the meditation exercise.

Signature: ....

DAILY QUESTIONS

1. What do you wish people knew about you the second they meet you?

....

....

....

....

....
....
....
....

2. When do you feel the happiest?

....
....
....
....
....
....
....

3. What could you never live without?

....
....
....
....
....
....
....

4. Why is it so important to you?

....
....

....
....
....
....
....

5. What gets you motivated?

....
....
....
....
....
....
....

6. How can you respect yourself more today?

....
....
....
....
....
....
....

7. How could you make someone's day better?

....
....
....
....
....
....
....

NIGHTLY READ:

Pumping Positivity in Conversations

Evening soldier!

I hope you had a great day. Tomorrow is the last day of the guide already! Doesn't time fly!? Going back on something I mentioned yesterday, I find it so funny how people always claim they don't have the time to do something when really, they do. I'm sure you thought you wouldn't have time to read a book and follow an entire 7 day guide with so many requirements including meditating twice a day, reading all these pages, answering questions and what not but, look, you did!

We make time for what we believe matters and we get to choose what matters.

I always use the excuse that I don't have the time to learn guitar or piano, I've been saying it for years. Same thing goes for learning how to dance - I had excuses when really I was just scared. It's just so entertaining to look back and think, "Damn, it's been 8 years since I first wanted that! Imagine I had started then, even just a tiny 10 minutes a day would have made me a piano player by now." It's just a quick thought to encourage you to start your goals now, even if the steps you take are tiny and seem powerless!

So let's get back to it, I want to talk about something completely different. I know this book is about you. I am making it a point to let you know that everything starts with your relationship with yourself. What do you think about yourself and what are more ways you can make yourself feel good? Have you ever considered how good it feels to give? That makes 'giving' sound selfish, haha! However, it really does feel satisfying to give. Something as small as opening a door for a stranger or exchanging smiles in public really can impact someone's day as well as your own. Asking people how they are with an intention to actually listen, rather than letting them talk just to blurt out your news and your own problems isn't really the same thing. I used to struggle with really listening to people but I worked on it and it feels amazing to help someone work through a problem towards a solution. Don't be afraid to give, to teach, to be considerate. It genuinely feels good. I like to sprinkle a little magic on the outside world; it has a ripple effect and definitely comes back to you full circle.

In saying that, I want to also express a method I use regarding my close family and friends. I have no idea where I got this from but it works for me. Be cautious of where your conversations always lead to. I created 3 optional rules I try to stick by. My conversations must be either:

1. Focused on positive news, progression of friends and family, ideas, plans etc.

2. Focused on a current problem, drama or issue. However, I make sure we are talking about ways to work towards finding a solution or making a plan.

3. Focused of venting about something even though we don't feel like we have any control over it because everyone needs a release despite knowing it will not resolve it.

In this third option, I stay aware that I won't allow this topic to be a recurring conversation in days, months and years to come if we aren't working on resolving it. My point is, keep the conversations constructive! If it is anything else, kindly change the topic even if you have to do it a few times on a few different occasions. It is easy to fall into gossip and that achieves nothing. I remember I used to talk people's ear off regarding my personal issues, such as my first heartbreak. That was normal and healthy of course, but the fact that I kept on going was so unproductive. It just gave power to the negative conversation and kept the past alive. I almost re-lived that pain everyday. I dramatically told stories and updated little pointless details. I gave the issue momentum and dragged it out far longer than I should have. My friends and family thought they were helping by buying into the conversations because I would make the stories funny and entertaining or at times dramatic where they craved certain updates on the drama. While I would have been upset if my people cut my conversation off cold turkey and told me to shut up, I wouldn't have been hurt if they just swayed the conversation away from that topic and kept redirecting towards a constructive conversation. It isn't on unhealthy just for the person talking; it is unhealthy for the listener.

Once you become aware of this you will begin to monitor how often you have pointless and draining conversations with people whether you were the one talking or listening. Give your time, focus and energy to topics and scenarios that can help you, not hurt you.

So in summary, have fun with sharing love. Get your excited bounce back in your step, find motivation and be the good energy that walks into the room. Help where you can, smile and ask people how they are but also be mindful of your conversations with your closest friends and family. Be the one who is guiding and influencing everyone to have more constructive and positive conversations without them even noticing. Once you become aware of this, you will begin to notice how often you were having pointless and draining conversations.

DAILY SUMMARY:

A Moment of Self-reflection

Write below a collection of thoughts or experiences from today. It can involve triggers you noticed where your mood almost changed (or did change), what you're proud of, or how you could have handled it differently. Things you enjoyed about your day or things that may have not gone to plan. Monitor how you're currently reacting as well as how you would like to learn to react. This should just be a diary form entry for you to keep track of your habits, progress, or areas requiring some self-reflection. Let it all out!

....

....

....

....

....

....

....

....

....

....

....

....

....

....

....

....

....

....
....
....
....
....
....
....
....
....
....
....
....
....
....
....
....
....
....
....
....
....
....
....
....
....
....

EVENING MEDITATION:

A Way to Clear Your Mind

(*You may wish to skip reading if you're already familiar with the instructions*)

This meditation exercise is the same as the morning meditation. Unless you're already familiar with the instructions, please refer to the morning meditation.

Please sign below if you have completed the meditation exercise.

Signature: ....

NIGHTLY THOUGHT

"Positive conversations feel good and I am

excited to have more of them!"

DAY 7

MORNING READ:
Cultivating Patience and Forgiveness

Hey there!

You've made it to your final day. I hope you had a great sleep and managed to grab this guide before you grabbed your phone. Do you feel it yet?

Do you feel a little different, a little lighter? More in control perhaps?

Remember, we give momentum to the thoughts and feelings we focus on, so make it a deliberate effort to keep this movement going in the direction we want it to go. Today will be as amazing as you allow it. I want you to decide that today is going to be a great day regardless of what you endure. It doesn't matter how outrageous things get, I want your mindset to filter out everything negative and to choose to give your attention to what is good. Stay positive, stay aware. When there are problems, struggle, or pain, focus on the hope and bring your attention to a solution. It is up to you to stay on track throughout your life. Let downs are natural, sickness and death happen, it is part of this amazing journey we are blessed to experience.

It is up to you to take the beauty from life, take the lessons and use them to better yourself as a person. When things happen to us, we have a decision about how we react. We have a moment to decide what this occurrence means to us. Do you want to decide to be mad at the world? Do you want to sit there and allow yourself to feel like the victim, or do you want to make it a goal to hold your head high and your heart open through the challenge?

If someone is rude or disrespectful, we must continue to be loving. This doesn't mean you need to go hang out with a murderer or buy the school bully a present, haha! It means, you need to remember that responding in anger only brings us more pain. Forgiving someone, is just as big of a deal for yourself as it is for the person you're forgiving even if they are no longer alive. To resent or to be revengeful is to simply weigh yourself down and no one wants to feel heavy.

People who hurt you are always hurting internally and what they say or do to you says a lot more about their relationship with themselves than it does about you. We must learn to be deliberate in acting out of love and that starts with self-love.

Respect yourself enough that you will not lash out at someone, or respond to hate with more hate. As much as a little road rage may feel good, or an angry impressive text to your ex-lover may poetically impress your friends, it is only hurting yourself. You are only emphasizing lower vibrating energies and accepting this reality into your life. Notice how you're responding to your past and how you're handling your present. Today is a new day, a new opportunity and I hope you make a decision that it will be a beautiful day, even if it's decorated in madness.

MORNING MEDITATION:

A Way to Clear Your Mind

It is now time to do a 7 minute meditation. For those who are experienced, you can get started as you already know the deal. For the beginners that are new to meditation, make sure to turn all electrical devices off or on silent then lay down on your back or sit upright in a comfortable position with your eyes closed for the entire duration of the music. It is important to find a relaxing position so you have the best chance at not shuffling and moving around during your meditation.

The goal is to have both your body and mind still. It may be a little unusual at first but you will notice the difference with ease by day 7.

You will naturally have thoughts pop into your mind but it is your duty to let them pass - watch them like clouds in the sky and don't focus on them. Do not give them power to start worrying you. In these short 7 minutes, you are allowed to let all your worries go; all your concerns and the things you have to get done are not welcome! Be still, breathe, and release your air deeply and slowly notice each muscle relax.

Please pull up the supplied audio and enjoy on all platforms! (See INDEX PAGE, page 134, TO LOCATE MUSIC)

Please sign below if you have completed the meditation exercise.

Signature: ....

DAILY QUESTIONS

1. What words of advice would you give your younger-self if you ever have the chance?

   ....

   ....

   ....

   ....

   ....

   ....

   ....

2. What is one positive thought that you have been thinking lately?

   ....

   ....

   ....

   ....

   ....

   ....

   ....

3. What would you do today if tomorrow wasn't going to exist?

   ....

   ....

   ....

....

....

....

....

4. What opportunity would you love to receive or attract if you got the chance?

....

....

....

....

....

....

....

5. How do you think you could be more likely to receive opportunities like the one above?

....

....

....

....

....

....

....

6. What are you excited about?

....

....

....

....

....

....

....

7. What are you grateful for?

....

....

....

....

....

....

....

NIGHTLY READ:

Establishing Consistency

So here you are - your final read. Don't hesitate to venture back and recap any part of this book. I'm hoping after you finish the 'Diary Outro' below, you can then check the first 'Diary Intro' paragraph of how you initially felt. I hope you have found some stillness after completing this guide. I hope to have given you some new tools alongside a new perspective to consider applying to your life.

Happiness truly comes from within and resonates outward. Learning to understand your triggers, what gets you upset, how to control your emotions regardless of the outside world, and understanding how to find spiritual peace within yourself is constant work. However, it can be enjoyable work if you stay on top of it. Just like your physical strength, you cannot take a 4 week boot-camp workout and get excited by the weight dropping off you yet return back to your old careless diet and expect to look and feel the same when you have stopped working out. You will end up where you started, or perhaps in worse shape - however, you'll know the work it took to improve your situation whenever you decide to try again next time.

Keep your emotional muscle memory strong too! A little work goes a long way and you deserve to feel light and joyful at all times. You deserve to smile and be in a mindset where you focus mostly on the good things and highlight the beautiful parts of life as you're walking down the street.

You must remember, you find what you're looking for! You notice more and more of what you focus on.

You attract what you allow yourself to feel! See the world through a pair of positive eyes and you will notice positivity. Prioritize your emotional health. Be the person who impacts others' mood and spreads the right type of energy. Lift your vibrational energy to a high place and keep it there! Take note of what vibrations come with the people around you. Have the courage to make changes and leave your comfort zone!

I hope that you have found some peace within this guide and that you have considered the spiritual perspective on life that I have spoken about. Please suggest this guide to others who you feel may benefit from the tools it holds inside and just remember, you are made of love, you deserve to smile, to love and be loved. I'm sending you love and energy now to go live an amazing life. There are no limits. Take care!

DAILY SUMMARY:

A Moment of Self-reflection

Write below a collection of thoughts or experiences from today. It can involve triggers you noticed where your mood almost changed (or did change), what you're proud of, or how you could have handled it differently. Things you enjoyed about your day or things that may have not gone to plan. Monitor how you're currently reacting as well as how you would like to learn to react. This should just be a diary form entry for you to keep track of your habits, progress, or areas requiring some self-reflection. Let it all out!

....

....

....

....

....

....

....

....

....

....

....

....

....

....

....

....

....

....

....
....
....
....
....
....
....
....
....
....
....
....
....
....
....
....
....
....
....
....
....
....
....
....
....
....

....
....
....
....
....
....
....
....
....
....
....
....
....
....
....
....
....
....
....
....
....
....
....
....
....
....
....
....

EVENING MEDITATION:

A Way to Clear Your Mind

(*You may wish to skip reading if you're already familiar with the instructions*)

This meditation exercise is the same as the morning meditation. Unless you're already familiar with the instructions, please refer to the morning meditation.

Please sign below if you have completed the meditation exercise.

Signature: ……………………………

NIGHTLY THOUGHT

"I'm going to kindly smile at random people tomorrow and see how many people I can bring a smile to their face."

<u>Optional Activity 3</u>

(Colour me in)

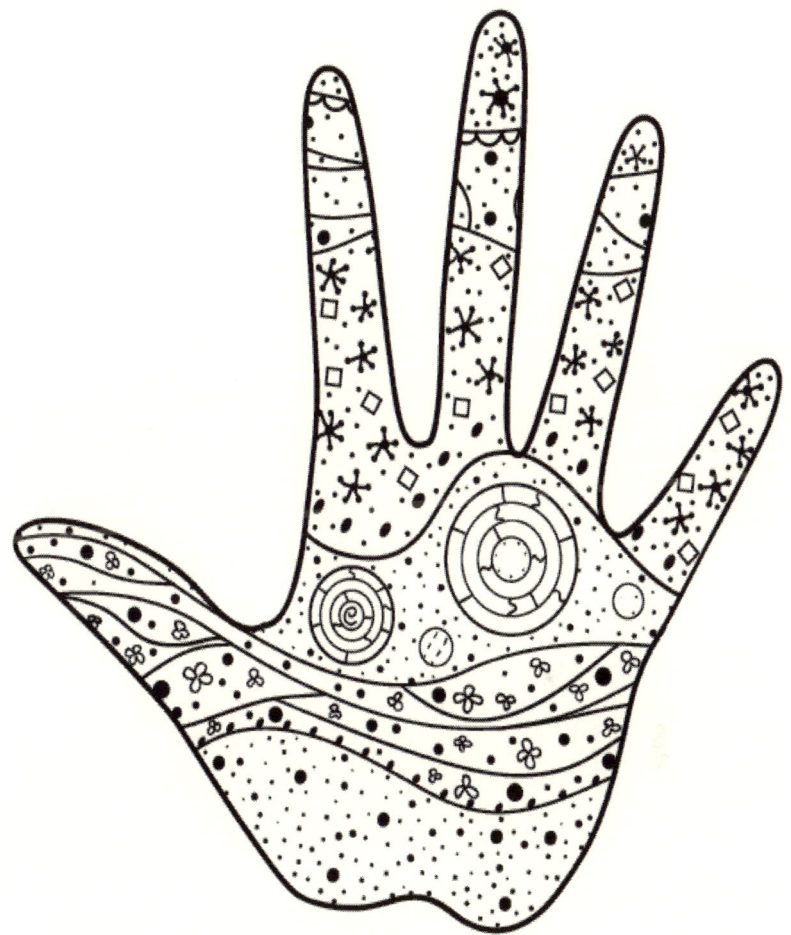

OUTRO DIARY LOG

The time has come; you have completed the 7 day guide! Now it is time for you to jot down how you're currently feeling and what you're experiencing. Imagine you have a chance to go back in time and to convince yourself to read this guide, or to encourage yourself to look into ways to change your current emotional status and to stop accepting feeling stressed, anxious or depressed on the daily. What unexpected discoveries, concepts or emotions have you found that your past self would be motivated by?

Explain things you have absorbed - helpful tools that stuck in your mind; any positive changes in your emotions that you discovered and anything else that comes to mind that would encourage your younger self to believe in positive change. This journey of self-understanding is lifelong and this outro will be a great journal entry to come back to if you ever want to remind yourself that you are able to influence change in your life.

Once you have completed the outro diary log below, it will also be a great opportunity for you to compare your feelings and circumstances to your initial diary log intro. Hopefully you will see a positive change.

Feel free to repeat this guide as often as you feel is needed and to suggest it to a friend or family member. I want to hear all about your experiences and to genuinely thank you for supporting this guide. You have the power to change your life; you have the ability to decompress!

....

....

....

....

....

....

....

....

....

....

....

....

....

....

....

....

....

....

....
....
....
....
....
....
....
....
....
....
....
....
....
....
....
....
....
....
....
....
....
....
....
....
....

....
....
....
....
....
....
....
....
....
....
....
....
....
....
....
....
....
....
....
....
....
....
....
....
....
....
....

INDEX

Meditation music link:

https://lnk.to/learningenergy